RAILWAYS

BY

COLIN

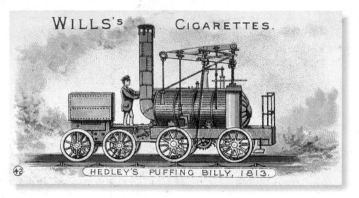

'PUFFING BILLY'

Many early locomotives stayed on the tracks by having grooved driving wheels which slotted into grooves in one of the rail tracks. The British engineer William Hedley designed train wheels so that there was sufficient grip between smooth wheels and smooth rails without the need for grooves. In 1813 he built a train called *Puffing Billy* using this new design. It was used to carry coal from a mine in the north of England to a nearby river.

CUGNOT'S STEAM CAR

Experiments with steam engines were not just taking place in Britain. In France Nicholas Cugnot, a military engineer, produced the first moving vehicle powered by steam. In 1769 he produced a three wheeled car for the French army to move cannons. The weight of the huge copper boiler at the front made it difficult to steer and on its first trip it ran into a stone wall. The next year Cugnot built another machine which he demonstrated in Paris. It turned over as it tried to turn a corner. Cugnot was arrested as a public nuisance and his machine was impounded.

TREVITHICK'S EXPERIMENTS

Richard Trevithick contributed to the development of the locomotive by being the first person to put steam-powered vehicles on to rails. He learnt his trade working for the owners of tin mines in Cornwall, England. As the mines were dug deeper and deeper the problem of draining them became greater. Trevithick developed a steam engine to pump water from the mines. He built his first steam-powered locomotive in 1801. It was demonstrated on Christmas Eve and pulled a number of people up a steep hill. In 1804 he built his first railway locomotive for an ironworks at Coalbrookdale in Shropshire. In 1808 he decided to show one of his trains in London. He built a circular track in Eaton Square, one of the most fashionable parts of London, and charged people to travel in a carriage pulled by the train. The locomotive did not catch the public imagination and Trevithick failed to get any interest in this new form of transport. He returned to his native Cornwall and continued working on stationary steam engines, including a steam threshing machine and the first rock-boring machine.

The First Steam Railway

ehicles that travelled by rail existed long before the arrival of the steam train. From the sixteenth century wagons were being pulled along wooden rails at mines throughout Europe. Grooves cut into the paved roads of the ruined city of Pompeii show that primitive horse-drawn railways existed even during the time of the Romans. This made travelling much easier since the wheels rolled along a smoother surface. However, it still relied on the muscle power of humans or animals. As a means of transport it was slow and could be used only for short distances. Although steam power was understood by the ancient Greeks, effective steam engines were not built until the middle of the eighteenth century. At first steam was mostly used to power stationary machines. It was only through the vision and determination of engineers in Britain and France that steam began to power the railways. Fast and long-distance travel then became a reality.

'CATCH ME WHO CAN'

One of the reasons why Trevithick's trains were an improvement on earlier steam-driven vehicles was that he found a way to put the steam in the engine under high pressure. This meant that the steam engine could be more powerful without making it bigger. Trevithick used a high pressure steam engine on the train he showed in London. The train was called 'Catch Me Who Can' by its passengers because it travelled on a circular track.

HAULING COAL

This steam locomotive was built by John Blenkinsop in 1812. It stayed on the track by means of grooves in the wheels and tracks. It was used to carry coal from a colliery to the city of Leeds, a distance of 3.5 miles.

Steam Locos' come of Age

'THE FLYING SCOTSMAN'

The *Flying Scotsman* is one of the most famous steam trains ever built. It was built in 1923 and travelled non-stop between London and Edinburgh, a distance of about 390 miles, even managing to change crew without stopping. At the time this was the world's longest non-stop run. It is claimed to be the first train to reach 100 miles per hour, although this cannot be verified.

The early attempts at steam-powered locomotion showed that it was possible to travel at speeds and distances that, until then, could only be imagined. Two British engineers, George and Robert Stephenson (father and son), carried out further development work and went on to build reliable steam locomotives for customers all over the world. Within a few decades whole countries and entire continents were linked by railway lines. Journeys that once took several days through inhospitable territory could now be done in just a few hours and in safety and comfort. The steam locomotive reigned supreme as the most common form of mass transport until the 1950s' when it was superseded by diesel and electrical power. The passion for steam trains carries on and many are still carefully looked after and run by railway preservation societies. There are also some parts of the world where steam trains are still being used on a commercial basis.

THE RAINHILL TRIALS

In October 1829 the owners of the Liverpool and Manchester Railway announced a competition to find the best locomotive for their railway. The five trains entered were either horse-drawn or steam-driven. It was won by the *Rocket* (shown left), largely designed by Robert Stephenson, (right). It travelled 70 miles at an average speed of 15 miles per hour. His victory also meant the triumph of the steam locomotive over horse power.

THE 'LOCOMOTION'

It was George Stephenson who convinced the
owners of the Stockton and Darlington Railway
to use steam trains instead of horse-powered wagons.
The first locomotive that he built for the railway was the
Locomotion, shown here. It pulled 28 coal-filled wagons.
For the first time there was a connecting rod between the
front and back wheels enabling them to turn together.
George Stephenson built three more locomotives for the
Stockton and Darlington Railway.

STILL USING STEAM

Steam trains are still being used commercially in several countries, particularly India and China.
This is because steam trains remain simple to operate and cheap to maintain. The cost of
replacing them with new diesel or electric trains can be very high. India still has nearly 5000
steam trains in operation and China has about 7000, more than the number of diesel and
electric trains combined. Zimbabwe repaired several of their old steam trains in the last years
of the 1970s because of the high cost of oil and
the lower cost of coal.

'THE BEST FRIEND OF CHARLESTOWN'

The first commercial steam locomotive that was built and used in the
United States of America was called *The Best Friend of Charlestown.* It first
pulled a passenger train over 6 miles on metal and wooden rails on
Christmas Day 1830. After running successfully for several months the
locomotive exploded. The engine's fireman had closed the safety valve
of the boiler because the noise of the engine annoyed him.

THE STOCKTON AND DARLINGTON RAILWAY

The Stockton and Darlington Railway in England was the first to use steam locomotives.
The engraving on the left shows the opening of the railway on
27 September 1825. With 25 miles of line laid it was
the longest railway in the world. It was built in an
area surrounded by coal mines and was soon
carrying over half a million tons of coal a year.
The poster on the right shows that the line
was also used to carry passengers. The first
passenger train was called the *Experiment* and
was a great success.

5

ON THE FOOTPLATE

There were always two crew members in the cab of a locomotive. The driver was responsible for driving the train and regulating its speed. The fireman had to see that there was water in the boiler and that the fire was kept stoked up with the right amount of fuel. Too much steam and the safety valves would shut down the engine to stop the boiler exploding; not enough steam and the train would stop.

EARLY IDEAS

This illustration comes from a book called *Mathematical Elements of Natural Philosophy Confirmed by Experiments*, printed in 1747. It shows that some people were thinking about using steam power for travel over twenty years before Cugnot built his steam car. It would have worked by heating up water in the boiler and producing a jet of steam. In theory this would have pushed the vehicle forward, an unlikely outcome. It would have needed a lot of fuel to produce enough steam to move the machine, and that would have made the vehicle too heavy. It took another two decades before it was realised that the steam had to be put under pressure before it could produce sufficient power.

HEATING THE WATER

In this cut-away picture of a steam locomotive there are lots of tubes running along the length of the locomotive. These tubes were surrounded by water. The hot gases from the firebox pass along these tubes and this heats the water and produces steam.

MOVING THE STEAM

The steam collects at this dome, called a regulator valve, and then passes along a tube to the pistons.

TURNING THE WHEELS

The piston is encased inside a cylinder. The steam enters the cylinder, pushes the piston forward which then turns the wheel. Each time the piston moves forwards and backwards the wheel turns through one revolution. As the piston goes back the steam escapes. More steam now enters the cylinder and starts the process again.

How a Steam Loco Works

The idea that steam could be used as a source of power had been around for centuries, long before the invention of the locomotive. In ancient Greece, Hero of Alexandria designed a machine that relied on steam power. However, it is generally accepted that effective steam technology really began in England in 1698 when Thomas Savery invented the 'Miner's Friend', a steam engine for pumping water out of mines. His invention was improved upon in the eighteenth century by Thomas Newcomen, James Watt and Matthew Boulton. By the end of the century steam engines were powering factories, mills and pumps both in Europe and America. It was Richard Trevithick who applied this technology to trains. Steam trains work by heating water to produce steam. The steam expands and the resulting pressure pushes a piston backwards and forwards. The moving piston turns the wheels of the train by means of a rod and crank connected to it. Although the design of the steam locomotive gradually improved, the way it worked has not changed significantly to the present day.

STEAM FROM A KETTLE

It is easy to see the principles of a steam engine whenever a kettle is used. The steam created by boiling water expands inside the kettle. As more steam is produced it is forced out under pressure through the spout.

NEWCOMEN'S STEAM ENGINE

This diagram shows the steam engine invented by the Englishman, Thomas Newcomen, in 1712. It was used to pump water out of mines. It worked by pushing steam into the cylinder. As the steam cooled it shrank and a vacuum was created. This pulled down the piston which raised the pump rods and removed the water. The piston was then raised by weights attached to the pump rods.

COUNTING THE WHEELS

Different kinds of locomotive are classified by the way in which their wheels are arranged. The small wheels at the front are called the leading wheels, the larger wheels are the driving wheels connected to the pistons and the back wheels are known as the trailing wheels. Many American locomotives had four leading wheels and four driving wheels but no trailing wheels. They were known as the 4-4-0 type.

'TOM THUMB'

In 1830 a race was held between a steam locomotive *Tom Thumb*, and a horse-drawn train. It took place on a stretch of the Baltimore-Ohio line. *Tom Thumb* broke down and the horse won the race.

CONFLICT WITH THE INDIANS

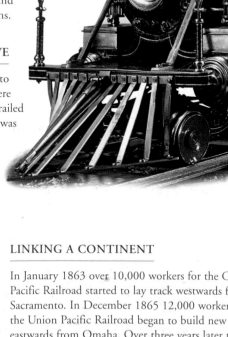

Many of the people who built the American railway system thought they were building on uninhabited land. In fact, they often laid track through territory that belonged to local Indian tribes. It is perhaps not surprising that the Indians saw the arrival of the railway, and the settlements that were built round them, as a threat to their way of life and attacked the trains.

AN AMERICAN LOCOMOTIVE

This train shows many of the modifications added to American steam locomotives. The bars at the front were called cowcatchers and protected the train from being derailed by large animals, like buffalo. Since much of the track was unprotected, a large lamp was placed at the front of the train to warn people of its approach. Early American locomotives used wood rather than coal as fuel for the firebox. A wire mesh had to be placed in the chimney to catch any burning wood sparks.

LINKING A CONTINENT

In January 1863 over 10,000 workers for the Central Pacific Railroad started to lay track westwards from Sacramento. In December 1865 12,000 workers from the Union Pacific Railroad began to build new tracks eastwards from Omaha. Over three years later the two lines met at Promontory Point in Utah. On 10 May 1869 the last spike, which was made of gold, was driven in and united the two tracks. It was now possible to take a train from the Atlantic to the Pacific coast of the United States of America.

American Railways

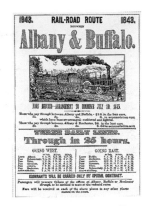

As railways spread across Europe they provided new links between cities and industrial centres. In the United States the story of the locomotive was very different. Railways were built through areas that had not yet been settled. Along these towns were created to serve the needs of the railway companies and their customers. The railways played an important part in opening up and developing many parts of the country. The expansion of the American railway system was massive. In 1870 there were about 53,000 miles of track in the United States. By 1900 this figure had jumped to over 190,000 miles. It reached a peak in 1916 when there were 254,000 miles of track.

THE RAILROAD CRAZE

The railways were successful in the United States because the public found it a cheap, fast and reliable way to travel. In the early years railway companies made more money from passengers than from freight.

THE 'STOURBRIDGE LION'

In the early years of the steam locomotive, American railways were dominated by English engineers and factories. Between 1829 and 1841 over 100 locomotives were imported into the United States from England. One of the first of these was the *Stourbridge Lion* for the Delaware and Hudson Railroad which began work in 1829. It proved to be too heavy to run effectively.

THE 'DE WITT CLINTON'

The first locomotive in New York State ran on 9 August 1831. It was called the *De Witt Clinton*. As the picture shows, passengers travelled on the inside and outside of the carriages. It was named after the politician De Witt Clinton, who died in 1828 after being senator, mayor and governor of New York.

Railways Reach the World

After Robert Stephenson won the Rainhill Trials in 1829 with the *Rocket* news of this exciting new form of transport began to spread round the world. People from many nations came to Britain to see and try it out. When they returned home they were determined to set up their own railway systems, but for many years Britain dominated the railway industry. Like the United States, many countries began by buying British-built trains. It was also British engineers who travelled round the world to supervise the laying of railway lines. After a while other countries began to build their own locomotives or to modify the trains they had bought so that they worked better in local conditions. By the middle of the nineteenth century the United States and Germany emerged as major competitors of Britain in the building of locomotives for the world market.

SWISS MOUNTAINS

Ordinary locomotives could not cope with the steep gradients in the Swiss mountains. In 1882 a Swiss engineer invented the Rack Loco shown here. It worked by having a toothed wheel which slotted into a grooved central rail.

THE 'CRAMPTON'

The type of train trapped in the snow in this picture was known as the *Crampton*. These British-designed trains were very popular in Europe, particularly France. The first public railway line in France was opened in 1837 and ran between Paris and St. Germain. From the 1850s the French railways adopted the *Crampton* engine. They were so successful that many people referred to rail journeys as 'taking the Crampton'.

GERMAN TRAINS

At the beginning of the nineteenth century what is now modern day Germany consisted of a collection of small states. The picture shows the first train to run in the state of Saxony. The first train in any of the German states was the British-built *Der Adler* which ran in 1835 between Nuremberg and Fürth.

AN IMPERIAL RAILWAY

Since India was controlled by the British, much of the track, locomotives and other railway equipment was supplied by British companies. The first Indian railway line was opened from Bombay to Thana on 18 April 1853, a distance of 25 miles.

TRAVELLING THE CONTINENT

After independence in 1947 the railway companies in India were nationalised by the government. Trains were modified to take account of local conditions. Like early trains in America, the train in this picture has a cowcatcher and a powerful lamp.

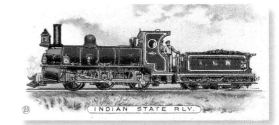

BREAKING UP AFRICA

In the mid-1880s the major European powers met in Berlin to carve up Africa between them. Each of the areas developed its own railway system. When the African states gained independence they found that twelve different gauges of track were in use. The train shown is a Beyer-Garratt locomotive used by Nigerian Railways. The first railway in Nigeria ran in 1901.

STEAM ENGINES IN JAPAN

The first train in Japan ran on 12 June 1872 from Yokohama to Singawa. The line was extended to Tokyo by October 1872. From 1880 to 1890 the Japanese railways grew from 98 to 1459 miles. In 1992 there were over 14,500 miles of track.

CHINESE RAILWAYS

This picture shows the first railway in China. It opened in 1876 and ran between Shanghai and Wuzong, a distance of 20 miles. It was only after the Chinese revolution in 1949 that railways in China began to expand rapidly.

Building a Railway

ISAMBARD KINGDOM BRUNEL

One of the greatest railway engineers of the 19th century was Isambard Kingdom Brunel. He started work with his father building the first successful tunnel under the River Thames in London. In 1833 he became engineer for the Great Western Railway and supervised the laying of the line between London and Bristol. He continued to build railway lines in England and Wales, including two railway bridges at Saltash and Chepstow.

Building a railway is not as simple as just finding the shortest distance between two points. As the Swiss railway builders discovered, trains could not climb steep hills or mountains. This was solved by either building the railway round the mountain, which saved money but lost time, or by carving a passage through the mountain, which saved time but cost more money. The first railway tunnel was built in 1826 on the Manchester to Liverpool line and was about one mile long. The longest railway tunnel in the world is the Seikan tunnel in Japan which is about 33 miles long. To cross rivers and valleys railway bridges also had to be constructed. The earliest railway bridge was built on the Stockton to Darlington line in England in 1824. The longest bridge in the world today is the Huey P. Long Bridge in New Orleans and is over 23,000 feet long. The work of the railway engineers and designers, such as Isambard Kingdom Brunel, is rightly remembered, but it is important not to forget thousands of ordinary labourers, some of whom lost their lives in the process, who also contributed to these lasting monuments to modern engineering.

BLASTING THROUGH ROCK

During the early years of railway building labourers had to cut through solid rock using only picks and shovels. It was the work of Alfred Nobel who finally made this part of railway building much less back-breaking. Nitro-glycerine is a liquid that is very unstable and highly explosive. In 1867 Alfred Nobel managed to make it stable by mixing it with a porous solid and so made it safe to use. He called his new invention dynamite.

FOREIGN LABOURERS

Railway building required a lot of workers and many railway companies relied on foreign labourers. This photograph shows American railroad companies using Chinese labour. Chinese people came to California during the 1850s and worked as unskilled labour. It is estimated that 10,000 Chinese labourers built the railroad over the Sierras and Rockies.

CROSSING THE RIVER

Because railways were built across all kinds of territory it became necessary to build different kinds of bridges. A normal beam or arch bridge might not be adequate for a train crossing a very wide river or valley. The Forth Railway Bridge which linked Edinburgh and Dundee and is pictured on the right was opened by King Edward VII in 1890. It was one of the first cantilever bridges to be built. Cantilever bridges are made of tubular steel towers joined together by a series of cables and brackets.

PAYING FOR THE RAILWAY

The building of the railways was often financed by governments because they realised their importance to the economy of the country. Money was raised by issuing government shares. When somebody bought a share they became a part-owner of the railway company and shared in any profits made. Governments were also involved in ensuring sufficient land was available for the railways. Today, many railway lines are owned by the state or receive government subsidies.

TOOLS OF THE TRADE

This picture from 'Punch' magazine is called 'Navvy in Heavy Marching Order' and shows many of the tools used by the men who built the railways. Alongside the pick and shovel there is a hod for carrying bricks and a small wheelbarrow to carry away rocks. The word 'Navvy' came from 'navigators'. Labourers employed to dig the first canals were called 'internal navigators'. Some were later employed to build the railways. Many of these labourers came from Ireland. Labourers who had helped to build the railways in Britain were used during the Crimean war in 1854. They helped build a small railway and dig trenches.

PULLMAN COMFORT

In 1859 an American industrialist called George Pullman experienced a very uncomfortable train journey. He decided to design a coach in which people could 'sleep and eat with more ease and comfort than on a first-class steamer'. He built the first modern sleeping car, the *Pioneer,* in 1863. He also built the first dining-car in 1868.

EARLY PASSENGER COACHES

This picture shows one of the earliest passenger trains. The coaches were converted horse carriages. Those riding on the outside were often covered in smoke.

SLEEPING IN COMFORT

Pullman began to sell his sleeping cars to England in 1873. They became very popular and well-known for their luxurious compartments. However, he was less successful in Europe because in 1866 a Belgian, called George Nagelmackers, after seeing a Pullman car in America, started to build sleeping cars for Europeans. His first sleeping car started running in 1868 and was called the *Mann Boudoir Sleeping Car.*

MODERN COMFORT

With increasing competition from aircraft and cars, many modern trains now have to offer a wide range of services to attract custom. This train has a cinema screen built into it. Heating and air conditioning ensure that whatever the weather outside the passengers inside remain comfortable.

ROYAL TRAINS

The sumptuous interior of this train shows that many European monarchs had their own carriages built. Queen Victoria of Britain had a luxurious coach with thick carpets and padded walls. It is said she enjoyed her sleeping-car more than her palaces.

Passenger Comfort

When the railways were originally built they were designed simply to carry goods for short distances. Railway companies soon realised that they could also make money by offering trains as a cheap and convenient form of transport for travellers. Later they realised that they would attract a larger number of people if they offered more comfort. This became essential in the United States as trains covered vast distances and people had to sleep on them. The railway companies began to offer different levels of passenger accommodation at varying prices. Those who paid the most went 'first class' and were given the most comfortable seats, more room and the smoothest journey. 'Second Class' passengers paid slightly less, compartments were smaller and less comfortable. These two classes of railway travel still exist on many railway lines. In the early years there was also a 'third class', often a roofless carriage without seats.

THE 'ORIENT EXPRESS'

For many the most luxurious train of all was the *Orient Express*. It first ran on 5 June 1883 and linked Paris and Bucharest in Romania. In 1889 it continued past Bucharest to Constantinople, now called Istanbul. After 1919 it included Italy on its route to Turkey. Its last journey was in May 1977.

EARLY SLEEPERS

The Canadian Pacific Railway offered sleeping accommodation to everybody, not just the wealthy. These beds were far less comfortable than the beds offered by Pullman.

DIFFERENT CLASSES

This picture from 1845 called 'Going to the Derby' shows the different kinds of service given to railway passengers. The picture at the top shows first class passengers about to enter their spacious carriage. The second class passengers in the middle picture had less leg room. However, they did have both seats and a roof which the third class passengers in the bottom picture had to do without.

Railway Stations & Signal Boxes

As passengers began to use trains to travel from one place to another, it became clear that they needed some kind of platform and shelter while they were waiting for the train, and assistance to board it since the doors were well above the ground. In 1835 in the German town of Nuremberg a wooden shelter was placed over a raised wooden platform. This became the world's first railway station. The first major railway station was Euston in London which was built at the end of the 1830s. As the nineteenth century progressed railway stations became larger and more ornate, using large amounts of steel and glass. Railway companies employed the best architects and engineers to design their stations. The largest of these were rightly called '*Temples of Steam*'. As the number of lines; and the number of stations continued to grow it became increasingly important for the trains to be controlled in some way. Collisions between trains happened often in the early days of steam. Railway companies employed several methods to ensure that both the trains and the passengers travelled not only comfortably but also safely.

SIGNALLING ARMS

One of the earliest ways of passing messages to the drivers of moving trains was by signalling arms that worked as a kind of semaphore. The upper arms tell the driver whether a train should stop or not. The lower arms are an advance warning for the next set of signals. The signal in this picture is telling the driver to carry on with caution.

WILLS'S

FIVE-NEEDLE TELEGRAPH IN

TICKETING

In the 1840s the first tickets for train journeys were issued. These were copper discs with the destination of the passenger engraved onto it. Only later did paper tickets with greater detail start to be used. Tickets were checked by guards and later by machines.

NEW STATIONS

Even though the importance of the railway has declined in importance with the rise of the motor car and the aeroplane, projects to build grand railway stations continue today. The picture is of D'Herouville station in Lyon, France. Building these stations encourages people to return to the railways and helps redevelop run-down areas in cities. They are still seen as symbols of the importance of a city.

GRAND CENTRAL TERMINAL

New York City's Grand Central Terminal was designed by Whitney Warren and constructed in 1907-13. It cost $43 million to build, which was a considerable amount of money at the time for a large public building. It could not be called a '*Temple of Steam*' because it was built to be used only by electric locomotives.

KEEPING IN TOUCH

It was important that signal boxes could warn each other of any problems in their block. The telegraph, invented in 1837 by William Cooke and Charles Wheatstone, was first used by the railways in 1839 to connect Paddington in London with West Drayton, a distance of just over 13 miles.

EARLY SIGNAL BOX

Railway lines were split up into "blocks" and each block was controlled by a signal box. The levers inside the signal box controlled the arms on the signals and also controlled the points. This was done by cables seen at the bottom part of the picture. These led from the signal box to the various signals and points within each block.

MODERN SIGNAL BOX

Operating the signals and railway lines has now been taken over by modern computerised systems. The screens show the positions of all the points, or junctions, where trains can change lines, the signals and the location of any trains in the area. The signals and points are controlled electronically.

Freight & the Railway Post

HAULING GOODS

The train above is operated by Amtrak, the American railway company, and is able to pull a large number of freight carriages. By the 1930s, diesel and diesel-electric locomotives had become more powerful than steam locomotives and could take far more freight. Many governments are concerned about the amount of freight on the road which causes congestion and pollution. They are trying to encourage companies to use railways to move their goods.

Well before the invention of the steam locomotive, horse-drawn trains were used to pull a few goods wagons. These were usually used at coal mines and travelled only a short distance to a nearby river or canal. When the steam locomotive appeared it suddenly became possible for trains to pull far more than just two or three carriages. As railway lines spread two more things happened. First the goods that they carried could be taken far greater distances and so cut out the need for the journey by water. Secondly trains began to carry not only raw materials like coal but also finished goods from the factories to the towns. Although the carrying of freight by train is less important in Europe and America, many Asian countries still depend on freight trains. One of the items most successfully carried by trains was mail. The first special postal train was introduced in February 1855 between London and Bristol. Before this time letters were carried by mail-coaches along muddy roads and were very slow and unreliable.

STILL USING STEAM

There are many parts of the world where not only is the steam engine is still the main source of power for freight trains and the dominant way of moving goods around. This is especially true of large countries like China, where this picture was taken. Behind the locomotive are the freight wagons called flat trucks, the simplest kind of wagon. The other main types of freight wagon are tank-wagons which carry liquids and container wagons which protect goods from the weather.

EARLY FREIGHT TRAINS

Early freight steam trains used the same carriages as horse-drawn trains. The train moved slowly because none of the carriages had brakes. When this problem was solved in the 1870s the trains could travel much faster.

FOLLOWING IMPERIAL ROUTES

The first railway lines built in Asia served the interests of the Europeans who controlled these areas rather than the native inhabitants. This meant that passenger trains were less important than freight trains. As this picture shows, countries like India still rely on the lines and the trains built in the early part of this century.

SORTING THE MAIL

Collected mail was taken to a special carriage where the mail was sorted into pigeon-holes. Once the letters had been sorted they were dropped off at designated stations. This was done without the train stopping. The mail was hung over the side of the train and caught by a net on the railway platform. The bags were then taken away for delivery.

PICKING UP THE MAIL

Trains were able to pick up any letters to be collected without the train having to stop. Letters waiting to be picked up were put into a bag and hung from a special hook as shown in the picture. As the train sped past a net suspended from the side of the train caught the mail bag.

Electric Trains

*L*ike steam, the potential of electricity as a source of power was understood many years before a practical use was found for it. In 1800 the Italian Alessandro Volta invented the battery which gave a constant supply of electricity and in 1819 the relationship between electricity and magnetism was discovered by the Danish scientist Hans Christian Oersted. Two years later the English scientist Michael Faraday built the first electric motor. Electric motors work with magnets. An electrical current passes along a coil which creates a magnetic field. This acts against the magnet in the engine and makes it spin. It is this spinning magnet that runs the engine. The first electric train was demonstrated by Thomas Davenport in America in 1835. In 1842 an electric train ran between Edinburgh and Glasgow in Scotland. It's top speed was 4 miles per hour. But it was another 37 years before the first serviceable electric train was built.

WERNER VON SIEMENS

The inventor of the first practical electric train came from a family of engineers and inventors. His electric train was first shown at the Berlin Trades Exhibition in 1879. It ran on an oval track about 300 yards long at a speed of 4 miles per hour. In 1881 the first public electric train ran near Berlin.

ELECTRIC TROLLEY CAR

This rather extraordinary electric train ran for 3 miles on rails on the beach between Brighton and Rottingdean in the early 1900s. It was built by Magnus Volk. He was also responsible for the first electric train to run in England. It first ran on 4 August 1883 in the seaside town of Brighton.

ELECTRIC TRAINS IN AMERICA

The first electric train to operate in America was introduced in 1895. In June of that year a passenger service near New York using electric trains ran for a distance of 7 miles. The train shown here is the first freight train to use electricity. It first ran on 4 August 1895 on the Baltimore & Ohio Railroad for a distance of nearly 4 miles. Almost half of this journey was through tunnels which was why electricity was chosen rather than steam.

IN THE CITY

Trams have run on city streets for many years and were first pulled by horses. Steam locomotives were not welcome on the streets of many cities because of the noise and pollution they caused. The arrival of the electric train meant that trams in many cities could be developed. For safety reasons they are usually powered by overhead cables and a pantograph, like this Japanese tram. Trams are one of the most important forms of public transport in the world's cities.

THE TGV

One of the fastest trains in the world is an electric train. The TGV (*Train à Grande Vitesse*) first ran between Paris and Lyon in France from September 1981. By 1988 the TGV was reaching speeds of over 200 miles per hour (320 kph).

RECEIVING POWER

This picture of a Siemens electric train at the Paris exhibition of 1881 shows how some electric trains received their power. On the top of many trains there was an arm known as a pantograph which collected electricity from overhead cables. Other electric trains took their power from a third "live" track that was laid next to the tracks that the train ran on.

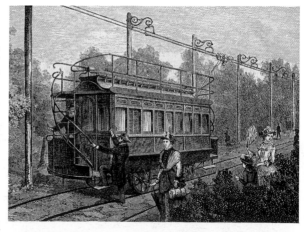

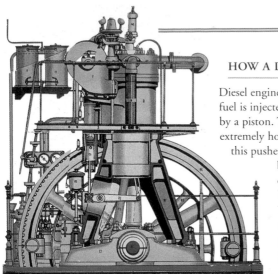

HOW A DIESEL ENGINE WORKS

Diesel engines work using a system known as fuel injection. Heavy diesel fuel is injected into a cylinder. The air inside the cylinder is compressed by a piston. The compression caused by the piston makes the air extremely hot. This causes the fuel inside the piston to catch light and this pushes the piston forward. The power of the engine is controlled by the driver varying the amount of fuel that enters the cylinder. On diesel trains the piston is then driven back by the revolving rod and crank attached to wheels. This compresses the air inside and the whole cycle starts again. In diesel-electric trains the piston powers a dynamo which produces the electrical power needed to turn the wheels.

THE 'DELTIC'

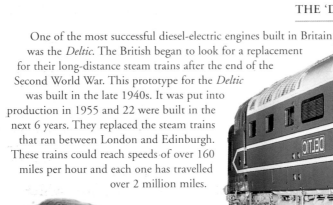

One of the most successful diesel-electric engines built in Britain was the *Deltic*. The British began to look for a replacement for their long-distance steam trains after the end of the Second World War. This prototype for the *Deltic* was built in the late 1940s. It was put into production in 1955 and 22 were built in the next 6 years. They replaced the steam trains that ran between London and Edinburgh. These trains could reach speeds of over 160 miles per hour and each one has travelled over 2 million miles.

RUDOLPH DIESEL

There is some dispute about who was the first person to invent the diesel engine. Some people claim it was first built by Herbert Stuart Akroyd in 1890. However, most people agree that it was a French-born German engineer named Dr Rudolph Diesel who invented the diesel engine. Between 1880 and 1890 he searched for an efficient replacement for the steam engine. He first demonstrated the diesel engine in 1893 but it was not until 1897 that he was able to build the first really reliable engine. In 1913 he disappeared overboard while crossing the Channel to England.

Diesel Trains

The third major source of power for trains is the diesel engine. A diesel engine is a type of internal-combustion engine that has many similarities with a petrol engine. Diesel trains were first used on an experimental basis in 1912 by the North British Locomotive Company. They were first used regularly the following year in Sweden. Diesel began to be used in America after 1923 and saw regular service in Britain after 1931. Between them, electric and diesel trains now dominate railways all over the world. Diesel engines are used either to power the engine of the train or, more usually, to run a generator which then produces an electric current. This then drives an electric motor. These trains are called diesel-electric locomotives.

HIGH SPEED TRAVEL

In 1957 the members of the European Community created an international network of fast and reliable trains. The TEE (*Trans Europe Express*) was an attempt to fight off the competition from airline companies. It was aimed at business people and had only first class carriages. These trains are all powered by diesel engines.

LACK OF ELECTRICITY

There are many countries where it is not practicable to replace steam trains with electric trains. This is because there are many lines that are not used very often and it would be simply too expensive to buy electric trains and the overhead cables that are needed to run them. Diesel is the preferred replacement.

THE DOMINANCE OF DIESEL

Since diesel trains are relatively cheap to buy and run it is not only in developing countries that diesel is the most popular replacement for steam. The American railroad company, Amtrak, has nearly 24,500 miles of track, only 344 of which are electrified. In 1994, 318 trains ran on these tracks. 65 of these are powered by electricity and 253 use diesel engines.

Great Train Journeys

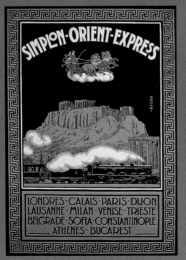

THE 'ORIENT EXPRESS'

For many the '*Orient Express*' (see p15) was the most glamourous of all train journeys. It has been the scene for many thrillers such as Agatha Christie's '*Murder on the Orient Express*'. There have been real life romances on board such as the millionaire Sir Basil Zaharoff falling in love with a Spanish duchess while travelling to Istanbul.

The building of railway systems throughout the world made many remote and inaccessible places easy to reach. Developments in railway engineering meant that there were no conditions which could not eventually be overcome. Deserts, forests and mountains, once impassable, were no longer obstacles to travel. Not only had it become possible to travel to new places but the train journeys themselves were spectacular, passing through some of the most awe-inspiring scenery in the world.

THE 'BULLET TRAIN'

This picture shows the *Shinkansen* running past Mount Fuji, a dormant volcano. The line between Tokyo and Osaka opened in 1964 and the trains travel at 160 miles per hour.

A TRAIN THROUGH AFRICA

The *Blue Train* runs between Cape Town in South Africa and the Victoria Falls on the Zimbabwean/Zambian border. The first luxury trains ran between Pretoria and Cape Town in 1939. It was only with the end of apartheid that it became possible for the train to continue through Zimbabwe and into the heart of Africa. It passes near Table Mountain, the diamond-mining centre of Kimberley, the Hwange Game Reserve, the Zambezi River and the Victoria Falls. It is one of the most beautiful journeys in the world.

ACROSS THE FROZEN WASTES

The Trans-Siberian railway runs from Moscow in the west to Vladivostock in the east. It is nearly 6,000 miles long and it takes an average of eight days to travel its entire length.

ACROSS THE ROCKIES

The first train to travel across the length of Canada set off from Montreal on 28 June 1886 and arrived at Port Moody a week later. It was later extended to Vancouver. Another transcontinental line was added in 1915 to the north of the first line. On this second line is the Quebec Bridge which is over 3,000 feet long.

THE 'HIAWATHA'

Nobody knows which steam train first reached 100 miles per hour. In 1893 an American locomotive claimed to reach a top speed of 112 miles per hour. Eleven years later in 1904 a train in Britain was supposed to have reached 102 miles per hour. Neither of these claims can be verified. The first train designed to run faster than 100 miles per hour was the *Hiawatha*. This train began service in 1935 and ran between Chicago and Minneapolis/St Paul. It reached an average speed of 80 miles per hour during part of the 412 mile journey.

THE 'FLYING SCOTSMAN'

The *Flying Scotsman* is probably the most famous steam train in Britain. It was built in 1923 and ran non-stop between King's Cross station, in London, and Edinburgh. This was the longest non-stop run in the world. It was eventually withdrawn at that line in 1963, after 60 years' service. In 1988-89 it went on a tour of Australia where it set the record for the longest non-stop run for a steam train, a distance of 422 miles.

THE 'ROCKET'

The first successful steam train was the *Rocket*, built by Robert Stephenson in 1829. It established the supremacy of steam over horse-drawn trains by winning the Rainhill Trials. It remained working on the Liverpool and Manchester Railway until the end of 1830, when it was replaced by the *Northwestern*.

THE 'EVENING STAR'

The *Evening Star* was the last steam train to be built in Britain in March 1959, the year before all steam locomotives were withdrawn from Canadian Railways. It was built as a freight train but was also used as a passenger train. It was eventually withdrawn from service in 1966. Two years later, all steam trains were withdrawn from service on British Railways.

Great Steam Engines

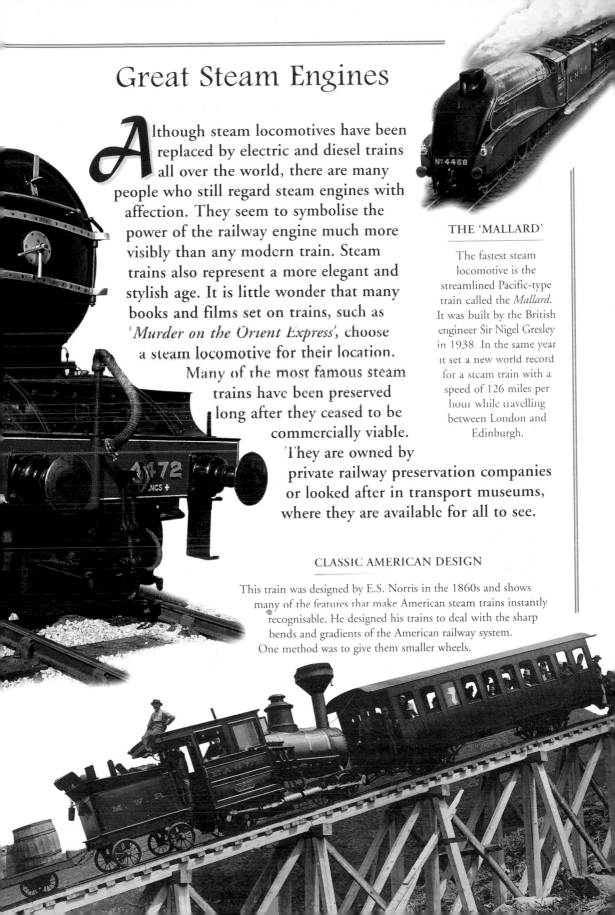

Although steam locomotives have been replaced by electric and diesel trains all over the world, there are many people who still regard steam engines with affection. They seem to symbolise the power of the railway engine much more visibly than any modern train. Steam trains also represent a more elegant and stylish age. It is little wonder that many books and films set on trains, such as 'Murder on the Orient Express', choose a steam locomotive for their location. Many of the most famous steam trains have been preserved long after they ceased to be commercially viable. They are owned by private railway preservation companies or looked after in transport museums, where they are available for all to see.

THE 'MALLARD'

The fastest steam locomotive is the streamlined Pacific-type train called the *Mallard*. It was built by the British engineer Sir Nigel Gresley in 1938. In the same year it set a new world record for a steam train with a speed of 126 miles per hour while travelling between London and Edinburgh.

CLASSIC AMERICAN DESIGN

This train was designed by E.S. Norris in the 1860s and shows many of the features that make American steam trains instantly recognisable. He designed his trains to deal with the sharp bends and gradients of the American railway system. One method was to give them smaller wheels.

THE MOSCOW METRO

The Moscow Metro is seen as one of the most opulent underground systems in the world. But there was a price. It was built in the early years of the 1930s at the order of Joseph Stalin, the Soviet leader, and was opened in 1935. Many of the labourers were prisoners. The work was hard and it is believed that thousands died while constructing it.

SMOKY TUNNELS

This picture from 1863 is an early picture of a train running on the London underground. It shows what appears to be a clean tunnel. The fact that steam trains were used meant that travelling on the underground was an unpleasant experience. This problem was partly solved by a special mechanism that diverted smoke into the water tank. By the end of the 19th century the use of electric trains on underground systems meant journeys became much cleaner.

CUT AND COVER

This picture from 1868 shows how the underground railway in London was constructed. It used a system called 'cut and cover'. A hole was dug, the brick arches of the tunnel were built and the hole was simply covered over again.

CONFUSING MAPS

The first maps of the London underground were difficult to understand. In the 1930s an engineer in London called Harry Beck created a new map. The stations were linked by straight lines and the central area was much larger than if drawn to scale.

Londoner (proud of the Tube system, to friends from the country). "THERE'S THE WHOLE THING, YOU SEE! *ABSOLUTELY SIMPLE!*"

Travelling Underground

One of the effects that the steam locomotive had on major cities was to allow people to live further from the centre of the city, where most of them worked. The suburbs of many cities were created as a direct result of the railway. This expansion caused its own problems as the streets of the city centres became congested with people and traffic. The ideal solution came in 1863 with the building of the first underground railway system in London. It ran from Paddington to Farringdon Street, a distance of nearly four miles. The success of the underground system in London encouraged other cities, concerned about congestion in their own streets, to build similar systems. Today the rise of the motor car has given rise to new environmental concerns and many cities are putting more money into their underground railway systems.

SQUASHED IN TOKYO

The underground system in Tokyo, which opened in 1927, is perhaps best known for the trains being so congested that people are employed to push passengers into the carriages to make sure that as many people as possible can be squeezed in.

AMERICAN SUBWAYS

This picture shows people entering a subway train in New York. Although the subway in New York is certainly the largest underground system in the United States, with over 240 miles of track, it was not the first to be built in America. The first American subway was built in Boston in 1897. New York City opened its first subway in 1904.

THE PARIS METRO

The underground railway in Paris is called the *Metro* and was opened in 1900. The stations in the centre of Paris are very close together and can easily be identified. The distinctive station entrances were designed by a famous architect called Hector Guimard using glass and cast iron and are in the Art Nouveau style.

THE GEORGE BENNIE
RAILPLANE SYSTEM OF TRANSPORT

Swift
Safe
Sure

The Future

From the 1950s on, railways were fast becoming a relic of a declining industrial past. The rise of the motor car gave people a far more flexible form of transport. Airlines offered both higher levels of comfort and lower prices to compete with long-distance passenger trains. In Britain, for example, the amount of track has been cut by about half from 20,000 miles of track in 1950 to about 10,000 miles in 1990, and in the United States from 224,300 to 162,700 miles of track in the last 40 years. Yet in the past few years the train has begun to fight back. Recent technological developments mean that trains are becoming much faster and more reliable. Concerns about the environment have also made many governments look to the train as a better way of moving people.

THE RAILPLANE

In the 1920s there was an experimental train built by George Bennie near Glasgow in Scotland. The wheels ran along a suspended monorail that was placed above the train. The train moved along the track with the use of a propeller at the back which pushed it forward. Although the experiment was a success the train was abandoned because it was too expensive to develop.

GAS TURBINE TRAINS

Gas turbine trains work by mixing gas with air and igniting it. The air expands and escapes. This air then spins a rotor which provides the engine with power. The first gas turbine train was built in 1941 in Switzerland but was abandoned as too expensive to run.

TRAVELLING AT HIGH SPEED

Many high speed trains would need new tracks which can be very expensive. In Italy a high speed train called the Pendolino has been developed with a special tilting mechanism so that it can deal with bends in the rails. It runs on two lines, one between Turin and Venice and the other between Milan and Naples. It has a maximum speed of about 185 miles per hour.

ABOVE THE GROUND

One of the ways in which trains reduce congestion in cities is by using overhead monorails. There have been monorail trains for many years. The first one was built in Germany in 1901 and is still used today. Modern monorails are either powered by collecting electricity from the side of the rails or are Maglev trains. (see below).

UNDER THE SEA

The picture on the right shows that there have been plans to dig a tunnel under the Channel between Britain and France for many years. The Channel tunnel was completed in 1992. High speed trains carry passengers from the centre of London to the centre of Paris in about 3 hours. The above picture shows the two high-speed British and French trains – the Eurostar and TGV.

MAGNETIC TRAINS

Many railway companies are experimenting with Maglev trains. Both the train and track have magnets which levitate the train and pull it along using the principle that magnets either attract or repel each other. This Maglev train is in Japan on the Yamanashi Maglev test line. The line opened in 1996 and is over 26 miles long. The trains can run at nearly 350 miles per hour.

DID YOU KNOW?

Who was the first person to die in a railway accident? The Liverpool and Manchester Railway was officially opened on 15 September 1830. There were 8 trains ready to pull over 600 invited guests, including the British Prime Minister and the Duke of Wellington. Another of the guests was William Huskisson, the member of Parliament for Liverpool and an influential backer of the railway. He stepped out into the path of one of the trains and was killed and so became the first person to be killed by a train. The Austrian ambassador, Prince Esterhazy, was also nearly killed by a train.

Where railway passengers find it difficult to breathe? In South America there are train services that run through the Andes Mountain range which goes through Bolivia, Argentina, Chile and Peru. On the track between Lima and La Oroya at La Cima in Peru the train climbs to a height of 15,806 feet above sea level. The highest station in the world is at El Condor in Bolivia. At these heights the air is very thin and rarefied and carriages have emergency bottles of oxygen for any passengers who have difficulty breathing.

Where is the straightest piece of railway track? One of the most luxurious train rides in the world is the Indian-Pacific which runs between Perth and Sydney in Australia, a journey of 2,386 miles. The train is over 2,600 feet long and first class passengers have their own private rooms with bathroom and toilet. There is a point of the journey where the passengers travel in a straight line for 297 miles. This is the longest piece of straight railway track in the world.

Who were the first passengers to ride through the Channel Tunnel? Before the railway tunnel between Britain and France was officially opened on 6 May 1994 by President François Mitterand of France and the British Queen Elizabeth II. One year before on 3 April 1992, Queen Elizabeth's husband, the Duke of Edinburgh, was the first person to travel the length of the tunnel. On 29 January 1993 the new British ambassador to France, Sir Christopher Mallaby, also used the tunnel and became the first person to travel to his new post without ever leaving land.

Which countries have the smallest railway system? There are several countries in the world that have no railway system at all such as Bhutan and Rwanda. There are also some countries that have a tiny railway system. Lesotho in Africa and the tiny principality of Monaco have only 1 mile of track each. Even though railways in the United States have been declining over the past few decades, the United States of America still has the most track of any country in the world. In 1990 the American railway company had over 162, 000 miles of track.

How rail lamps were developed? The United States was the first country to put lamps on the front of its trains. In the early 1830s Horatio Allen, who started the South Carolina Railroad Company, placed a burning pile of pinewood in an iron basket on his trains. By the time of the Civil War in America most rail lamps used oil for fuel and had powerful reflectors to throw the light forward.

ACKNOWLEDGEMENTS

We would like to thank: Graham Rich, John Guy and Peter Done for their assistance.
Copyright © 1998 ticktock Publishing Ltd. Picture research by Image Select. Printed in Italy.
First published in Great Britain by ticktock Publishing Ltd., U.K.. All rights reserved.
No part of this publication may be reproduced, stored in a retrieval system, or transmitted in any form or by any means, electronic, mechanical, photocopying, recording or otherwise, without prior written permission of the copyright owner.
A CIP Catalogue for this book is available from the British Library. ISBN 1 86007 022 1

Picture Credits: t=top, b=bottom, c=centre, l=left, r=right
Ann Ronan @ Image Select; 2tl, 2l, 2br, 3b, 3tr, 4br, 5bl, 5br, 5tr, 5c, 6bl, 6tl, 6/7c, 7r, 7br, 8l, 9r, 9tr, 10tl, 11tr, 11tl, 12bl, 12tl, 12br, 13tr, OFC & 13br, 14tl, 15br, 16r, 17br, 19t, 20tl, 20bl, 21br, OBC & 22tl, 25tr, 28bl, 28br. Chris Fairclough Colour Library/Image Select; 7tr, 21r, 22br, 25cr, 29br. Colin Garratt/Milepost92½/Corbis; IFC1, OFC & 4/5c. Corbis/Bettmann; 9b, 12/13cb, OBC & 14c, 14cb, 27b. et archive; OBC & 22bl, OFC, 26tl & 32c. Forabolafoto (Milan); OBC & 30/31c. Hulton Getty; 15bl. Image Select; 2bl, 8bl, 8t, 11bl, 17cr, 21tr, 28/29c, 29bl. Mary Evans; 10l, OFC & 10b, OBC & 11br, OBC & 12/13c, 14tr, 18/19c, 19br, 31r. Michael Yamashita/Corbis; 31bl. Milepost 92½; 10/11c, 16br, 18tl, 23tr, 30bl. Pix; 14bl, 15tr, 16bl, 17tl, 25tl, OBC & 24tl, 29tr, 31c. Science and Society Picture Library; OFC & 4bl, OFC & 8/9c, OFC & 16tl, OBC & 22/23c, 27tr, OBC & 30tl. Spectrum Colour Library; 4tl, 24/25, 26cb, 26/27c, 26bl, 28tl. Trip/C Rennie; OFC & 20/21c.

Every effort has been made to trace the copyright holders and we apologise in advance for any unintentional omissions.
We would be pleased to insert the appropriate acknowledgement in any subsequent edition of this publication.

snapping-turtle
guide